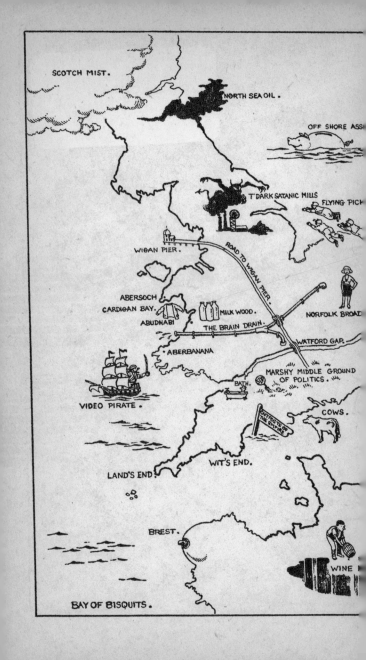

# Map of
## The Known World

# 1984
# AND ALL THAT

Also by Paul Manning
*and published by Futura*

**HOW TO BE A WALLY**

# *1984*
# *AND ALL THAT*

*Paul Manning*

Futura

A Futura BOOK

First published in 1984
by Futura Publications, a Division of
Macdonald & Co (Publishers) Ltd
London & Sydney

Copyright © Paul Manning 1984
Cartoons by Patrick Wright

ISBN 0 7088 2612 1

Typeset, printed and bound in Great Britain by
Hazell Watson & Viney Limited,
Member of the BPCC Group,
Aylesbury, Bucks

Futura Publications
A Division of
Macdonald & Co (Publishers) Ltd
Maxwell House
74 Worship Street
London EC2A 2EN
A BPCC plc Company

# CONTENTS

# POMPOUS FOREWORD

CONTINUING the work so ably begun by Messrs Sellar and Yeatman in their pioneering volume 1066 AND ALL THAT, the aim of this book is to present a concise, relevant, and, it is hoped, *memorable* history of the Twentieth Century, from its inception in the year *Nineteen-fourteen-eighteen* to the present day.

But (the reader may object) can a topic so vast *possibly* be encompassed in a book of a mere 128 pages, inclusive of author biography, contents page, printing and copyright details and the intriguing insert to be found at the end of all Futura paperbacks inviting gullible readers to send cheques and postal orders to a P.O. Box in Falmouth? The answer is: yes. Everything you can remember about the Twentieth Century is contained in this book. By the same token, *there is nothing in this book that you do not already know*.

1984 AND ALL THAT is a reassuring volume designed to fit snugly into the pocket or be carried around easily in the head. It is not, nor is it intended to be, exhausting. It is, however, so far as the author has been able to ascertain, the first ever guide to the Twentieth Century to contain all (or most) of the information judged to be memorable by all (or most) of the Great British People all (or most) of the time.

1984 AND ALL THAT easily supersedes all previously published works and is therefore the only one of its kind.

The rest are History.

# Part 1

## Nineteen-fourteen-eighteen
## And All That

# CHAPTER ONE

## *MODERN HISTORY BEGINS*

JUST as the first date in English History is 55 B.C.,* so
the first entirely relevant and memorable date in *Modern*
History is *Nineteen-fourteen-eighteen*, in which year the Imperial Splendours of Edwardian England were swept away for
ever by the First World War, or Great War to End Wars.
Thenceforward, all History up to that point was declared
irrelevant, and the Twentieth Century could at last begin.

The Great War was very important, as it changed the
face of Europe and resulted in a harsh Treaty signed in the
celebrated Hall of Mirrors, or Salle Boche, at Versailles.
The Treaty declared:

(a) That the war was all Germany's fault, so Germany
should be made to pay a fine.
(b) That Germany should not be allowed to re-arm,
except in secret.
(c) That the German wartime practice of eating babies
was atrocious and should cease forthwith.
(d) That several new Baltic States should be created,
e.g. Estonia, Latvia, Lithuania, Snowdonia, Belgravia,
etc.

*See *1066 And All That.*

(e)  That a cordon sanitaire, or chastity belt, be placed between Russia and Germany.

(f)  That some corner of a foreign field should be Forever England.

All of which was really a *Good Thing*, as it made the world Safe for Democracy.

*Forever England*

# CHAPTER TWO

# *THE POST-WAR WORLD*

T HE main British Statesman at this time was Lloyd
George, a very able politician who is nowadays chiefly
memorable for knowing everybody's father and also for his
remarkable private life. Such was his skill in managing the
affairs of state and having mistresses at the same time
(whom he confined in country cottages) that he was widely
credited with magical powers and thus became known as
the *Welsh Wizard*.

In the end, however, Lloyd George could not answer the
Irish Question* and was succeeded in the Twenties by
Bonar Law (who was prevented from becoming memorable
due to ill health). He therefore retired from History and
devoted his declining years to mistresses, country cottages,
etc., and propagating the Lloyd George Raspberry. He
was thus a Good Prime Minister but (probably) a Bad or
Weak Man.

### *Social Life in Britain*

In the Edwardian or Halcyon Days, life in Britain had
been quite old-fashioned, e.g. there was always honey for
tea, and murders were still done by gaslight. Society too
was strictly segregated and consisted of the Leisurely
Class, who lived *upstairs*, and the vast or bored mass of the
populace, who lived *downstairs*, in scullions and pantries.
However, after the war this was considered an outmoded
arrangement and abolished. (It would in any case have
become impractical eventually, owing to the invention of
the bungalow.)

*There is no answer to this.

During the war, women had worked very hard at making munitions, so many people felt they ought to be given the vote. Also, there had been many demonstrations about this by the Suffragettes, some early Feminists led by Mrs Emily Parkhurst, who were always chaining themselves to railings or setting fire to their corsets in Hyde Park. The Government therefore introduced the Representation of the People Act, thus giving the vote to everybody (except Peers, lunatics, felons, flappers, etc.) This caused Universal Suffering, and was, needless to say, a Good Thing.

CHAPTER THREE

## THE RISE OF SCIENCE

EVEN before the war and the birth of the Modern Era, there had been many very memorable breakthroughs in science. These enabled the people of the time to be considerably more civilised than their Forefathers, many of whom had been Rude. Marconi, for example, had invented wireless telepathy, which led to the famous arrest on board the *Titanic* of the notorious murderer Dr Stafford Crippen. This was closely followed by Dunlop's timely invention of the wheel, which in turn gave rise to the horseless carriage or infernal combustion engine and so spelt the end of the Handsome Cab, Bicycle Made For Two, etc. (At first, however, motor cars could not go very fast as they were vintage models and had to be preceded by a servant singing the red flag.)

*Rude Forefathers*

### Invention of Relativity by Einstein

Another very important scientific advance of the time was Einstein's Relativity. This was a very advanced theory which Einstein had first advanced in 1905; however, nobody seemed to understand it then, so Einstein put it on one side and advanced it again later, in 1916, when it was known as the General Theory of Einstein's Theory of Relativity. Nowadays the theory is not so advanced, and most scientists can understand it. It can be summarised thus:

(a) Absolutely everything is Relative (except for Ablatives, Rulers, etc., which are Absolute).

(b) Absolutely everybody's Relatives are Obsolete.

(c) Absolutely all Absolutes are Irrelevant.

(d) Everything depends on where you happen to be standing at the time.

These conclusions Einstein formulated in the memorable equation $E = mc^2$, where '$c$' is a consonant.

In spite of Einstein's breakthrough, by 1919 Science had still not progressed enough, so Rutherford had the idea of splitting the atom in the Cavendish Laboratory in Oxford. This had never been done before and was very difficult owing to the minute smallness of atoms, which can only be seen through a telescope, thus making it hard to tell whether the atom in question has been split or not. Rutherford, however, was utterly successful in splitting one and was later able to discover that atoms contain electrons, protons, photons, newtons and croutons, thereby paving the way for the dawn of the nuclear age, invention of nuclear family, etc.

## CHAPTER FOUR

# *THE RUSSIAN REVOLUTION*

AROUND this time the world was very shaken for ten days by the Russian Revolution. This, however, had to happen because Russia up till then had been very backward and even had a partly backward alphabet, and was still inhabited by fiery horsemen called Trossacks, who had been left over from the Crimean War and would charge up and down Steppes on their horses, waving sabres and uttering blood-curdling ululations.

The revolution began when some left-wing peasants and Volga boatmen decided to topple the Szar, or Tsar, whom they accused of standing in the way of progress and failing to give proper instructions on how to spell his name.

The Shar, it was alleged, had also let his wife, the Sharif, be hypnotised by Rasputin, who was a bad influence and was turning the Crown Prince Alexei into a homophiliac (or clot). (Probably the Cigar had also angered the revolutionaries by claiming to have been anointed by God, whom the revolutionaries, being atheists at this time, firmly believed to be dead.)

When he heard that the revolutionaries wanted to topple him, the Char became quite upset and declared he was strongly opposed to a revolution as it would clash with the First World War, which he happened to be fighting at the time. To try and avoid a confrontation, he therefore changed the calendars around and ordered St Petersburg to be renamed Petrograd, hoping that the revolting peasants would get confused and eventually give up and go home.

This, however, was a petrograde step, as on the 12th March (under the Gregorian Calendar) or the 27th February (under the Julian Calendar), the revolutionaries merely retaliated by splitting themselves into factions, thus confusing the Saar and causing either a Provisional government (which was reactionary) or a Retrograde Soviet (which was composed of Bolsheviks, Mensheviks, etc., and thus paradoxically progressive) or, according to historians, both.

While the Star was trying to work out which was which (if any), the Bolsheviks then stormed the Winter Gardens, and the Saab, realising his position was now untenable, wisely abdicated and was later cruelly assassinated in the Urinals.

### The Russian Civil War

The events of the October (or November) Revolution of 1917 (which of course took place in March [February] of

*assassinated in the Urinals*

that year) were so confusing to everybody that the Russians decided afterwards to hold a civil war to find out who had really won. This was fought between the Red Russians (Bolsheviks) who were Left, and the White Russians (Dons, Cassocks) who were Right – or rather, Wrong (in a way). In the end, however, the White Russians inevitably lost, due to not having History on their side.

Though the Russian Revolution was inevitable, even some Communists now admit that it was not entirely a Good Thing, as it led to Stalin, a very Bad Man who liquidised everybody and forced Trotsky to flee the country and be horribly done to death with a toothpick.

# *UP TO THE START OF THE TWENTIES*

1. Would the course of History have been substantially altered if instead of Bosnia, Herzegovina and Dalmatia being ceded to Yugoslavia, Rumania and Armenia had been ceded to Bukovina?
Does it matter?

2. What was the point of the Fourteen Points, Comment pointlessly.*

3. Expostulate imperiously on either
   (a) Imperial Preference, or
   (b) The incidence of plebiscites in Upper Silesia.

4. Eulogise aeronautically:
   (a) Hawker and Siddley
   (b) Alcock and Bull.

5. Why did Asquith never succeed in making the wearing of seatbelts in Hansom Cabs compulsory? Would this have been a Good Thing?

6. "He had a double dose of everything, good and bad."
To what extent is this a fair description of
   (a) Lloyd George?
   (b) Your father?

7. To the best of your knowledge, have you ever suffered
   from
   (a) Trench Foot?
   (b) Squiffites?
   (c) Smuts?
   (d) Friction in the Balkans?
   (Be honest.)

8. To what extent did the Lloyd George Raspberry
   represent a considered response to the Irish Question?

9. How can you be sure that a particle of light travels at
   186,000 miles per second? Is this safe
   (a) After dark?
   (b) In a built-up area?

10. Is there honey still for tea?

*Ballpoints may not be used.

# Part 2

# *The Twenties — A Roaring Decade*

When the Twenties began, everybody in Britain suddenly started behaving in a very roaring and unbridled way, throwing wild parties, athletically dancing the Charlton or Black Bottle, wearing very Twenties-style clothes, and throwing away their inhibitions. This could never have happened before, as inhibitions were quite a recent discovery by Freud (see p. 29) and it was not until the Twenties that people realised they had any.

The Twenties were, however, quite a Good Thing really, as they enabled the Thirties to be put off for another decade, and were also memorable for the discovery by Lord Carnavon of an Egyptian burial chamber on Tooting Common.

# Chapter One

## *THE BRIGHT YOUNG THINGS*

NOTHING better characterised the brittle spirit of the Twenties than the invention of a frightfully exclusive club in Park Lane called the Bright Young Things. The members of it were mostly rich young socialists who were exclusively frightful and were determined to be typical of the period by being madly Bright and Young, wearing silk dressing gowns and flimsy dresses known as *flappers*, smoking very daringly in public and also by practising birth control, which had just been discovered by Dame Marie Stopes and was currently all the rage.

The Bright Young Things were originally the Bright Idea of Noël Coward and Gertrude Lawrence and were later immortalised by the novelist Evelyn Waugh in her sparkling novel *Put Out More Bodies*. Waugh had once been a Bright Young Thing herself and set out the rules of the club in the following immortal declaration:

### DECLARATION OF WAUGH
(i) All members to be madly Bright and Young at all times.
(ii) All members to be madly Witty and Amusing and to avoid mentioning anything Mad or Old such as the Horrors of Waugh. (This would have been thought madly Dull and thus a Baugh.)

(*Note:* Evelyn Waugh should on no account be confused with the Great Waugh, or Waugh to End Waughs.)

# CHAPTER TWO

# *THE MODERN MOVEMENT*

*artistic capital of Europe*

IN the Twenties it was announced that it was now Paris's turn to be Artistic Capital of Europe. This caused many artists, writers and composers to flock towards it from all over the world in a great migration known as the *Modern Movement*.

The Modern Movement included such memorable names as James, Joyce, Ebeneezer Pound, Ernest Hemming, Gertrude Steinway, the Symbolists, Dadaists, Fauvists, Mauvists, etc., and was a Good Thing, especially from an administrative point of view, as it enabled everybody to be in the same place at the same time. (Also, it benefited the artists, writers, etc., as if they had not taken part in a movement they might not have been noticed by the critics.)

After the movement arrived in Paris, like all previous artistic movements it moved into the Latin Quarter, which had always been the favoured resort of artists, Bohemians and students wishing to improve their Latin. Here, the Modernists occupied tall apartment blocks, enabling them to write and paint meaningfully on many different levels, and proceeded to startle Parisian Society by making outrageous exhibitions of themselves in salons.

### The Bloomsbury Group

This was quite similar to the Modern Movement and was a group of writers consisting mainly of two wolves, Leonard and Virginia. These for some reason did not go to Paris, but instead met each year at the Chelsea Flower Show in Bloomsbury, where they became memorable for amongst other things formulating the Bloomsbury Rules, a gentle-manly and exquisitely civilised way of boxing.

### Picasso – a terrible painter

Picasso is often referred to as the *enfant terrible* of the Modern Movement, since he was terribly modern and shocking and had been an *enfant terrible* as a child.

*Blue Period*

Though Spanish, Picasso had begun his career by audaciously doing some French Impressionists at the turn of the century; these had been quite realistic, thus proving that he could paint properly if he wanted to. After this, however, his paintings became worse and worse and even Picasso himself became quite depressed about it, leading to his memorable Blue Period. Fortunately he soon gave up being blue and became a Cubist instead, thus changing the course of Twentieth Century art, after which he went on to paint some of his most famous and priceless original Picassos.

## CHAPTER THREE

# *SCOT FITZGERALD AND THE JAZZ AGE*

THE Jazz Age must be mentioned here, since it is often confused with the Roaring Twenties, and even at the time it was hard to tell which was which. In fact, the Jazz Age is easily remembered as it was the one begun by the memorable American Scot, F. Fitzgerald. This happened in the following way.

While on a visit to Europe with his wife Ella, Fitzgerald had been forcibly struck by the Roaring Twenties and was recovering in a Swiss Insanatory when he thought what a good idea it would be to start a similar period in America and set his novels in it. The idea was a great success, and the Jazz Age soon spread not only to Hollywood but to many playgrounds in Europe, e.g. the French Riviera, where it was even available in Cannes.

*The Freudian Slip*

After this, however, Fitzgerald's life took an unhappy turn, as he was a romantic at heart and had never much cared for Jazz anyway and was far more interested in popularising the Great Gatsby, a fashionable and rather romantic type of hat. In the end, he became one of Hollywood's many talented prostitutes and after futile attempts to extinguish himself in a typing pool, was one day tragically consumed in his own flames.

### Sigmund Freud

In the Twenties many people all over Europe and America began to have disturbing dreams of a symbolic or Freudian nature. This was due to the influence of the memorable psychoanalyst Sigmund Freud, who had recently set up his couch in an edifice complex in Vienna.

Dreams had of course been an established and recognised phenomenon since early times, but before Freud, people were mostly unaware of them as (a) The dreams emanated from the Unconscious, which Freud had not discovered yet; and (b) They were always asleep at the time.

Having already made a name for himself by shrinking the crowned heads of Europe, Freud later went on to invent an unintentionally revealing undergarment known as the *Freudian Slip*, which he claimed could be worn without the wearer even realising it.

# CHAPTER FOUR

# *THE GREAT STRIKE*

IN 1926, the Roaring Twenties were rather regrettably interrupted by the Great Strike in Britain. This was quite serious, and certain historians have claimed it could have led to a revolution. However, as every student of History must surely have observed, revolutions are mainly confined to the Continent and cannot happen in Britain, owing to the Good Sense of the British People, with their traditions of fair play, respect for Law and Order, constitutional monarchy, proper drains, etc.

The strike began when the miners asked for shorter working hours. The pit-owners, however, at first weakly refused on the grounds that normal working hours of sixty minutes were quite short enough and they did not want to have to alter all the clocks; they then changed their minds and agreed to grant shorter working hours, but only in return for a longer working day, at which point the miners stormed out in disgust and called a strike.

The Strike was a general strike, since anybody could join in (except, of course, the general public). In the end, however, it was a failure, for three reasons:

(i)  The workers could not agree how long it should go on for, which caused the Division of Labour.

(ii)  To overcome the lack of public transport, the public ingeniously bought bicycles, thus inventing Social Mobility.

(iii)  Hoping to enforce the strike, the workers posted pickets at factory gates, but these were never delivered as the postmen were on strike too.

*Results of the strike:* The Great Strike was in fact a Bad Thing for the workers, since after it the Government passed a very unpopular act known as the Trades Disputes Act. Also brought into effect at this time was the Breeding of Unnecessary Schoolchildren Act, which was to stop the workers having such large families, as these were a burden on the State.

## CHAPTER FIVE

## *PROHIBITION*

AT the beginning of the Twenties, a very interesting measure had been introduced in America known as *Prohibition*. This was a law which said that the people were not allowed to drink alcohol such as liquor or gin unless they drank it illicitly, in a speakeasy or in the bathtub, in which case it was all right and nobody minded. This was very moral, and also very American, as it encouraged private enterprise, e.g. when Charles Lindbergh flew the Atlantic in 1927 with a planeload of spirits from St Louis.

The most colourful figure of the Prohibition Era, however, was Al Capone, an Italian opera-lover, who, though poor, had pulled himself up by his bootlegs and become Chicago's top grocer and florist, specialising in wreaths, which he would always deliver in person. Capone was a very good businessman and invented an extreme form of insurance known as *Protection*, whereby he would call on his customers and ask if they needed protection; if the answer was no, he would then either shoot them or burn their house down, thereby proving that they did need it

*Al Capone*

after all. Capone was also on very good terms with policemen and politicians and is thought to have been the originator of *organised crime*. This was much more efficient than the old-fashioned disorganised kind and was thus obviously a Better Thing.

In the end, however, Capone went too far, surprising a group of business rivals in a Greek restaurant by leaping out of a serving dish armed with a tommy-gun and shooting them all – a disgraceful episode which is remembered to this day as the St Valentine's Day Moussaka.

The Wall Street Crash happened in New York in 1929 and is also known as the Great Crash, since it was one of the loudest ever recorded and broke the Dai Jones Index. The Crash should not, however, be confused with the *Boom* (though this was also very loud).

The causes of the Crash were as follows:

(a) *The Boom.* This went on far too long, thus making the Crash inevitable.

(b) *The Wall Street Bears.* Before the Crash, confidence was badly undermined because of some bears on the stock exchange floor who were selling shorts; this was of course illegal at the time due to Prohibition, and caused investors to become nervous.

(c) *The Bulls.* These rushed into the market because of the Boom and on noticing the bears, promptly stampeded, causing the foundations to give way and the bottom to drop out of the market.

Hearing the Crash, many speculators panicked and immediately flung themselves from the top of skyscrapers and were completely ruined. The Wall Street Crash was thus a very Bad Thing and brought the Twenties to a disastrous end.

# Part 3

## *The Thirties —*
## *A Dismal Decade*

The Thirties is without doubt one of the most dismal and dreary epochs of the Twentieth Century, since it contains amongst other things the Jarrow Crusade, the Rise of Hitler, the Abdication Crisis, Appeasement, the first Royal Christmas Day Broadcast, and the invention of Polythene. Sensitive readers may therefore, if they wish, be excused the following chapters altogether and have the author's permission to rejoin the narrative on p. 58 at the paragraph headed THE FINEST HOUR.

# CHAPTER ONE

## *THE SLUMP*

THE first dismal thing to happen in the Thirties was
when the British Government under Ramsay Macdonald was forced to introduce a Slump. This caused great
misery and hardship but nothing could be done about it as
it was caused by the world situation and was mostly to do
with Economic Factors, which could only be understood
by experts. For example:

(a) *Uncooperative attitude of Russia.* Ever since the Revolution, Russia had rather rudely refused to join in world
trade as it was too busy building 'Socialism in one
Country', viz. Russia. This had caused the end of *free
trade*, and from then on everybody had had to pay.

(b) *Outflow of capital.* During the Great War, capital had
flowed from Britain to America; afterwards America
had lent it to Europe and it had all flowed back again.
But when the Crash came, America suddenly stopped
lending it and asked for the capital it had already lent to
be given back as it was rather hard up due to the Crash,
whereupon Europe said it was too late as it had spent it
all. This was a Bad Thing as it meant that nobody had
any money any more.

### The Gold Standard

Another effect of the Slump was that Britain went off the
Gold Standard. The Gold Standard was a sacred cow that
was kept in the vaults of the Bank of England, and it was
always feared that if the cow was ever removed or lost, the
£ would go crashing through the floor and there would be

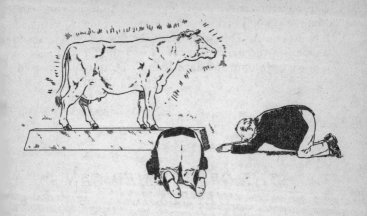

a terrible rush to get out of Stirling. Unfortunately, because of the Slump Britain was so short of gold that the cow had to be melted down for scrap. This was known as going off the Gold Standard, and in fact was not quite as bad as people had thought, since many economists had gone off it already.

### Keynes

During the early Thirties, the Macdonald Government could not remove the Slump because of *Laissez-Faire*, a law which dated back to the nineteenth century and which said that governments must never do anything about anything. Before long, however, everything became so bad that the Government realised it would have to do something. A remedy was therefore proposed by Lord Beaglebrook, a newshound on the *Express*; this was for the building of a vast Tariff Wall around the Empire, which he said would help the building industry and also raise money for the country, since foreigners could be charged 10% admission before being allowed through. Unfortunately Beeblebrox was found to be merely exercising the prerogative of a harlot and the idea was abandoned.

In the end, the situation was saved by the memorable Cambridge economist Professor John Milton Keynes of Cantab University, who around this time invented the Mixed Economy and wrote books showing the Government how to run it. This was one of the few Good Things to happen in the Thirties, as it caused the Government to remove the Slump and have Managed Capitalism instead.

CHAPTER TWO

## *THE GREAT AMERICAN DEPRESSION*

IN the early Thirties, everybody in America had lost all their money in the Wall Street Crash, and so suffered from the Great American Depression. The American Depression was very similar to the English Slump but was known as the Depression because it took place mainly in *depressed areas*, e.g. the Dust Bowl, a very dusty, flattish, deepish depression in the ground somewhere in Oklahoma. Indeed, some believe that the Depression started in the Dust Bowl, due to the failure of the grape harvest, which was because the farmers there did not know it was the wrong place to grow grapes. (The hardships of life during the Depression are very memorably depicted by John Steinbeck in his famous novel *A Handful of Grapes*.)

### *The New Deal*
At first nothing could be done about the Depression as America did not have a President. This was the fault of the last President, Calvin Coolidge, who, instead of being

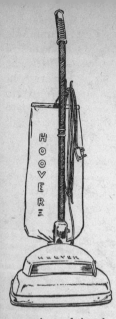

*Hoover*

assassinated in the normal way, had been accidentally swept out of office by a Hoover, thus creating a political vacuum (or Hoover Moratorium). In 1932, however, the Depression had become so bad that the Americans decided to replace the Hoover and elect a new president instead; Roosevelt therefore swept to power.

Franklin Delaney Roosevelt was a vigorous president and always showed great sympathy for the plight of the Little Man, or Small Farmer, who had always been at a great disadvantage in America owing to his diminutive stature. Roosevelt pledged to help him in any way he could and, on taking office, immediately showed great vigour for a hundred days by passing some measures known as the New Deal. Though not Fair (the Fair Deal was by Truman in the Fifties), the New Deal was a Good Thing as it said that (a) Nobody could sell apples on the sidewalk; and (b) Everybody should have a beer (End of Prohibition). This was very encouraging to the Americans and meant that America could go back to being the Land of Opportunity again.

*The Small Farmer*

### The Hollywood Greats

During the Depression, the people of America and of Britain flocked to the pictures, since it helped to take their minds off the Depression and also there was so little worth watching on the television. The films of this period were known as *Talkies*, to distinguish them from the films of the previous period, most of which had been silent (hence, the *Silent Majority*).

Many of the great films made at this time were classics and starred the great film stars of the Thirties, the Hollywood Greats, so named because of the Golden Age of Hollywood which was going on at the time. The Hollywood Greats lived in very grand mansions known as movie palaces, and were of course idolised by the Americans, since they were instead of a Royal Family, which the Americans can never have, due to their lack of History.

# CHAPTER THREE

# *FAILURE OF THE LEAGUE OF NATIONS*

THE League of Nations had originally been quite a good idea by the American President Woodrow Taylor in 1920, as it had been set up to stop the First World War happening again. However, in the Thirties it proved quite useless, due to its failure to stem the tide of Fascism, which was causing the storm clouds of war to loom very menacingly over Europe.

The League was a club which you could join if you had signed the Treaty of Versailles, and the rules were inscribed on a League Covenant which was kept in the League club-house in Geneva, along with various articles which members could make use of, such as peace treaties, League tables, declarations, law courts, squash courts, and international bar facilities. The club-house also contained some machinery for settling international disputes, but this was rarely used by members as they could not read the instructions, which for some reason had all been printed in Esperanto.

The rules of the League were:

(i)  No state on any account to start a World War. (This was now illegal.)

(ii)  No state to sack, loot, pillage, put to the Sword or violate the territorial integrity of any other state without asking first.

(iii)  No state to declare war on any other state without also declaring war on everybody else as well (the so-called Doctrine of Collective Insanity).

(iv) Any state held to be in breach of Rules (ii) or (iii), e.g. by sacking, looting, pillaging any other state, etc., to be requested to resign from the League. (State would thus be a non-member and no longer bound by League rules and could therefore carry on sacking, looting and pillaging in peace.)

However, though noble in intention, the League of Nations was too idealistic and thus could not prevent:

(a) *The Mancunian Crisis.* This occurred in 1931, when the Japanese accidentally invaded Manchester, thinking it was part of China.

(b) *Mussolini's invasion of Abyssinia.* Though this only happened in Africa it was quite important historically and showed Mussolini's utter lack of territorial integrity. After it, the Abyssinian King Highly Salotte was forced to seek refuge in Britain, where he was accorded the romantic title "Lion of Longleat".

## CHAPTER FOUR

## *DEATH OF GEORGE V*

IN 1936, King George V of England died, having been on the throne since 1910. He was, however, a very popular king as he had the hair of an old sea dog and was an occasional broadcaster on the wireless and his trousers were always creased *at the sides*, thus endearing him to the

British people. His royal consort was also very much loved, as she was the Queen Mary, also a keen sailor, who was very famous on both sides of the Atlantic for her stately bearing and unmistakable large red funnels.

George V's gruff good humour and love of the sea never deserted him, and even on his deathbed he showed his abiding concern for the fate of the British Empire by his very memorable remark, '*Bugger Bognor*'. When he died it was thus the end of an era, viz. the Georgian Era, and he was immediately succeeded unsuccessfully by Edward VIII.

### Edward and Mrs Simpson

Edward VIII was not at all like his father George V, as he was determined to be a thoroughly modern monarch. Indeed, he had begun as a thoroughly modern prince by cementing the ties of Empire with new cement and making some quite modern remarks about slums, miners, etc. However, by far the most startling sign of Edward's modern outlook was when he caused the Abdication Crisis. This occurred in the following memorable way.

While still a prince, the King had been conducting an affair of state with a certain Mrs Simpson, an American Lady, in the Belvedere, a small and select hotel in Windsor Forest. At first, this had been very hush-hush, so that only the rest of the world had come to hear of it. However, on ascending the throne, Edward immediately shocked the nation by announcing his wish to make Mrs Simpson his wife and if possible, Queen. The church and government leaders were outraged by this and declared it would be a very Bad Thing, since it was well known that Mrs Simpson was a divorced woman and thus unconstitutional. They therefore quickly invented a law known as the Common Law which said that the King could never marry anybody common, especially Mrs Simpson, and that in future Mrs Simpson must always have her divorces in Ipswich, so nobody would notice.

As Edward still insisted on the marriage, he was then compelled to denounce the crown, accompanying himself on an instrument of abdication, after which, disguised as the Duke of Windsor, he romantically fled the country with Mrs Simpson in a morganatic carriage, and was replaced by his brother George VI, thus causing the Georgian Era again.

The Abdication Crisis was a romantic episode in Britain's history and quite memorable, since it showed that even though it was now the Modern Era the British People really preferred the old-fashioned style of kingship and were thus only modern in parts.

<br>

## CHAPTER FIVE

# *ADOLF HITLER – REVOLTING BUT MEMORABLE*

<br>

UNFORTUNATELY at this stage in world history we cannot avoid encountering one of the worst and most odious characters of the Twentieth Century, namely Adolf Hitler. His vile deeds, however, must be recounted since they are, regrettably, *memorable*.

Adolf Hitler had revolting table manners and could never make a speech without foaming at the mouth, shrieking hysterically in a ridiculous German accent, and rolling around on the carpet in a frenzy. He was quite Mad, and had once been a Mad Corporal in the First World War, and lived in an eagle's nest in Bavaria. He is also memorable for writing his notorious diary, which was later exposed as a worthless forgery, since the paper he had written it on had not even been invented at the time.

He was thus without question one of the most uncouth and unspeakable of all historical figures and can only be described as a dastard.

Hitler was Bad from an early age, having been a Bad Painter in Austria in his youth. In 1923, he had been put in prison for showing some revolting tendencies in a Munich Bierkeller and punished by being made to write *Mein Kampf*. This, however, only made him worse, as it gave him his most dastardly idea of all, viz. to hold the First World War again and this time win it, thus making Germany *top nation*.

### Hitler's Rise to Power

Hitler's Rise to Power had begun as early as the Roaring Twenties, and one of the chief causes of it had been the Weimar Republic, a small, quite weak republic situated in Weimar at that time. This was famous during the Roaring Twenties for its unbridled decadence and cabarets, and also for its Roaring Inflation, which caused the people living there to light cigarettes with banknotes, travel to the shops in suitcases, and even sell their grandmothers in exchange for tins of cheap Ersatz coffee. (This is memorable as being one of the few times in history when grandmothers have been legal tender.) This was clearly a very Bad Thing and led to a Lack of Moral Fibre among the populace, thus making it very easy for Hitler to take them over.

Having seized control of the Weimar Republic, Hitler very soon became ruler of the rest of Germany too, by a variety of strong and infamous measures, as follows:

(a) *Making the trains run on time*. A strong measure, and popular with the Germans, who have always been sticklers for punctuality. Later copied by Mussolini, but less successfully, since the Italians were less punctual. (E.g. even when the trains were on time, the Italians were always late and thus kept missing them.)

(b) *Construction of the Siegfried Line*. Another strong measure, and quite necessary at the time, since before it

*The Siegfried line*

was built the German Hausfraus had nowhere to hang their washing.

(c) *The Hindenburg Disaster*. Finding his path to power blocked by Hindenburg, Hitler pronounced him a disaster and thus overcame him. A strong and infamous measure.

(d) *The Reichstag Fire*. A very infamous measure. On being refused entry to the German Reichstag, Hitler burned it to the ground, blamed the fire on the Communists, and was thus able to enter it by the back door.

(e) *The Nuremburg Rally* (or Master Race). Another strong and popular measure; this was a yearly cross-country event organised by the local Mastersingers, to see who could drive the fastest Volkswagen, a popular car invented by Hitler, which all Germans were made to own.

By these and other nefarious and unsavoury means, Hitler achieved absolute power in Germany and thus elected himself Chancellor of the Third Reich (the first two having ceased to be memorable some time before).

# CHAPTER SIX

# *CHAMBERLAIN AND APPEASEMENT*

AT this time, the British Prime Minister was Neville Chamberlain. Though extraordinary in being the first flying Prime Minister, Chamberlain was in every other way utterly ordinary and had once been Mayor of Birmingham. Another example of his extreme ordinariness was his Umbrella, which he always carried with him wherever he went, in case of the Gathering Storm in Europe.

One day, hearing that Hitler was about to annex the Sudetenland, Chamberlain decided to make a flying visit to Munich with his Umbrella in order to tell the German dictator that this would be all right. This was known as the policy of Appeasement.

The visit seemed a great success at the time, as Hitler was successfully appeased by it and agreed to sign a great peace with Britain known as the Peace with Honour, or more usually, the *Peace of Paper*. This was a promise by Hitler (a) Not to try and enlarge his living room, as it was quite large enough already; and (b) Never to rape Czechoslovakia, Poland, the Low Countries, the rest of the world, etc.

*enlarge his living-room*

However, as soon as Chamberlain had flown back to Britain, Hitler immediately changed his mind and decided to (a) Enlarge his living room; and (b) Rape Czechoslovakia, Poland, etc. This gave incontrovertible proof of his Badness, and caused something to go wrong with the lights, which immediately went out all over Europe.

# *UP TO THE END OF THE THIRTIES*

1. "It was not the League that failed but the nations."
Confute with reference to the use of short-acting
barbiturates in intravenous anaesthesia.

2. Compare soporifically:
    (a) The Great Sleeping Sickness epidemic of 1922
    (b) Orwell's *Homage to Catatonia*

3. Which British statesman, after a visit to Glasgow in
1925, "sat down on a pin and howled"?

4. Would you describe Stanley Baldwin as:
    (a) A superb professional?
    (b) Honest but stupid?
    (c) Blinking but sniffing?
    (d) Neurotic but spiffing?
    (e) All four?

5. Examine the role of Sidney and Beatrice Webb in the
development of
    (a) Fabian Socialism
    (b) The Webbs Lettuce.

6. Consider the significance of (a) Teapots, and (b)
Domes, in the political career of Warren G. Harding.

7. What convinces you that Calvin Coolidge was ever
    (a) Alive
    (b) Dead
    If (b), how could you tell?

8. Clarify by means of sketch-maps, flow-charts, Venn Diagrams, Critical Path Analysis, etc.,
   (a) The Road to Wigan Pier
   (b) The love-life of H. G. Wells.

9. Do not attempt to perform a Quantum Leap, but instead write not more than three lines illustrating the proposition that sub-atomic particles are dangerous and should only be handled by qualified Quantum Mechanics.

10. 'Chamberlain's policy of Appeasement failed to provide a lasting peace in Europe *because* . . .'
    Complete the above sentence in words of not less than ten syllables.

    (Candidates are advised to write on one side of the question only.)

# Part 4

## *The War Years*

This book has up till now been quite neatly divided up according to decades. The War Years, however, rather annoyingly do not fit properly into either the Thirties or the Forties, since they are from 1939 to 1945 inclusive. For the sake of convenience they have therefore been given a *Part* of their own; this is roughly half a Part (the War Years lasting roughly half a decade). The half decade 1945–50 is also covered in a Half Part, i.e. Part 4½: *The Post-War Years*. Part 5 is normal.

By far the most relevant thing to happen during the War Years was *The War*. Indeed, the War Years were almost exclusively taken up with it, and anything else that happened during them is generally regarded as Irrelevant. It was thus exceptionally memorable and affected the whole world, even quite inferior or Low Countries such as Belgium, which are by tradition Irrelevant and can never normally play any significant part in History.

# CHAPTER ONE

## *THE BALLOON GOES UP*

I N the Thirties, many people had foolishly pretended that the Second World War would never happen. However, in 1939, it could no longer be prevented, owing to the dreadful behaviour of Hitler, who was by now invading people in all directions and was clearly bent on planting his heel all over Europe, thus becoming Absolute Ruler of Absolutely Everybody. The final act of provocation came when Hitler very dastardly let off a balloon from the roof of his Chancellery in Berlin; this caused the balloon to go up in Europe, where it was immediately spotted by the British with the help of Radar, which had just been invented by Barnes Wallis. The Second World War therefore officially began.

*Winston Churchill*

The main cause of the British eventually winning the war against Hitler was Winston Churchill, who was the last of the Bulldog Breed and also the last Wholly Great Englishman, those who followed being at best only Partly Great. As well as being Great, Churchill was quite a Good Bad Painter and painted a very memorable portrait of himself by Graham Sutherland (later destroyed by his widow). Throughout his life he was excessively fond of Brandy and fat cigars, which never harmed his health as when he died he was very old and was only suffering from natural causes, for which reason he has ever since been the patron saint of smokers and drinkers.

Churchill, however, was not always Great, and at first it seemed he would not be very Great at all; for example, during the First World War, when he was voted Worst Sea Lord of the Admiralty, due to the Dardanelles Campaign. He was also quite unpopular during the Thirties as he was always predicting the Second World War and saying it was inevitable; however, nobody believed him, thus making war inevitable. These prophetic utterances later caused him to be termed a *Cassandra*, a type of blind Greek sightseer.

### Churchill takes command

When the war broke out, Churchill immediately showed his Greatness by declaring that Hitler was a Bad Man on the Home Service and that the war was therefore 100% Right and a Good Thing, thus causing a wave of patriotic fervour to sweep the land. He also wasted no time in placing the Nation on a War Footing, e.g. issuing the people with gasmasks, War Footwear, etc., and warning them to be on the lookout for enemy spies and paratroopers. These were in fact easily recognisable since they always carried heavy suitcases and went around the country disguised as nuns.

CHAPTER TWO

# *THE PHONEY WAR*

SOON after the commencement of hostilities, Hitler had the very treacherous idea of tricking the British by means of the Phoney War. This was so called as it was fought in a very phoney, insincere way, e.g. the bullets in it were not real and the soldiers were allowed to get up again after they had been shot. It was thus not a proper war at all but an imitation one. The British and French, however, did not realise this and were so busy incorrectly fighting it that when Hitler suddenly started the Real War they were taken completely by surprise. This, of course, actually showed their natural superiority, since it had never occurred to them that Hitler would stoop to such a shabby trick.

BANG

Hitler then continued his unfair tactics by pressing westwards into France, overrunning the Maginot Line (thereby bringing services on the French Metro to a standstill) and once more surprised the British by bringing his tanks up by the wrong route, i.e. through the Belgian Ardennes, which was in fact impossible because of the trees there, thus eventually causing them to be caught in a rather nasty Panzer Movement.

### The Miracle of Dunkirk
This took place in 1940 at eleven o'clock, when the British Army found that they could not defeat Hitler yet as it was only 1940, and thus became stranded at Dunkirk, and only

a miracle could save them; whereupon, learning of their plight, the ordinary people of Great Britain (and the Navy) immediately miraculously saved them by going down to the sea in ships (and in some cases, cars), thus effecting a miraculous eleventh-hour rescue. Dunkirk thus was one of the most stirring and memorable wartime exploits of all time, and not a defeat at all, and was particularly stirring and plucky because it was done by the ordinary people (and the Navy), and because the ships used in it were mostly only Little Boats, e.g. fishing smacks, cockleshells, saucy ketchups, etc. (except the ones belonging to the Navy). This showed the native British genius for improvisation and proved that the Britons of 1940 were the rightful ancestors of Sir Francis Drake, Sir Walter Raleigh, Alfred the Cake, etc.

## CHAPTER THREE

## *THE BATTLE OF BRITAIN*

THE British were in fact bound to win this, owing to their air superiority. Hitler, however, did not know this, and having by now defeated everybody except Britain, thought he would defeat Britain too and thus win the war. Naturally, this move was fiercely and valiantly resisted by the British, since a German victory at this stage would have been quite unhistorical, and so the Battle of Britain inevitably began.

At first the battle seemed grossly unfair and unequal, consisting as it did of the entire German Luftwaffe versus

*The Few*, a very small handful of Battle of Britain Aces. However, this was actually to the British advantage since it enabled the Few to fight against overwhelming odds, a circumstance which throughout History has never failed to produce a British Victory. Also, the place chosen for the battle was the Field of Human Conflict, a field near Biggin Hill, Kent, which again favoured the Few, as if they baled out, they were not so far from home.

*Field of Human Conflict*

*However, without doubt the main cause of the British Victory was . . .*

## THE FINEST HOUR

Even Historians do not know exactly when this occurred, except that it was probably sometime at the height of the battle. However, as soon as the British pilots noticed it, they became very inspired and showed extraordinary skill and courage and went on to decisively win the battle. This was a glorious feat, as it showed the invincible British spirit, and caused Hitler to give up trying to conquer Britain and start trying to conquer Russia instead.

# Chapter Four

# *AMERICA ENTERS THE WAR*

Aᴍᴇʀɪᴄᴀ was late for the War, owing to Isolationism, and probably would never have joined in at all but for the memorable cowardly intervention of the Japanese, who one morning around this time very cowardly sailed into Pearl Harbour while all the Americans were asleep and thus easily destroyed the U.S. Fleet. This, however, was a Good Thing as it led to *the Allies* and thus brought closer the historic *Allied Invasion of Europe*.

### *The Longest Day*

The invasion of Europe was very momentous and memorable as it took place on the Longest Day, or D-Day for short. The Longest Day was so-called as it was extremely long and lasted all day, thus giving the Allies time to swim the Channel with a giant Mulberry, scale the Atlantic Wall, stage an ambiguous landing at Normandy (or alternatively, Calais) and there take the defending German forces by surprise. This proved very effective, the Germans being so startled (particularly by the Mulberry) that they immediately became confused and did not know whether the invasion was really at Normandy or Calais (or vice versa). As a result, they were soon overcome, and from then on, Hitler's days were numbered (e.g. D+1, D+2, etc.)

## The Battle of the Bulge

By now, Hitler had become quite weak and dissipated through having exposed himself on too many fronts. However, to everyone's surprise, he struck back boldly in the Bulge, a distended part of Belgium, ordering his troops to open fire along the *Ghost Front*, which the American GIs refused to defend as they thought it was haunted. This could have caused a defeat for the Allies had not General McAuliffe, the U.S. General, ingeniously sent the Germans a card bearing the word 'NUTS', which once more threw the enemy into utter confusion, enabling the Americans to blow up their fuel dumps and thus causing the German Army to be demobilised.

### Defeat of Hitler

The downfall of Hitler came right at the end of the War, when the Allies, having successfully crossed the Siegfried Line, quite openly and in full view of the Germans, *hung their washing on it*, thus signalling a crushing Allied Victory and precipitating the complete collapse of the German war effort.

When he heard the news, Hitler flew into a great rage and became more mad than ever. Then, realising that he had failed to make Germany top nation, he madly assassinated himself in the bunker along with his notorious henchmen and caught the first U-boat to South America. Whereupon the Second World War at long last came to a .

*hung their washing on it*

# Part 4½

## *The Post-War Years*

By the expression "Post-War Years" is meant here the years Nineteen-forty-five to fifty. These can be dealt with quite briefly, as they are in fact shorter than the war years as not so much History happened in them (or if it did, it is not very widely known and thus cannot have been Relevant.)

# Chapter One

# *THE ATTLEE GOVERNMENT*

*naked into the debating chamber*

THOUGH he was a great wartime leader, Winston
Churchill could not be so great in peacetime, and so
when the war ended, he let Clement Attlee be P.M.
instead. Attlee quickly formed a government consisting of
Morrison, Dalton, Cripps, Staffs., Morrison Morrison, and
including the memorable blunt Welshman Nye Bevan (not
to be confused with Nye Bevan), who once startled
delegates to a Labour Party Conference in Brighton by
going naked into the debating chamber.

64

Attlee at this time passed a number of very worthwhile Acts and is also memorable for inventing an extremely valid policy known as the National Insurance Policy. This gave the people a feeling of social security, as it said that if ever the nation was lost, stolen, accidentally burnt down, damaged by frost, earthquake, fire, flood, civil commotion or Act of God, the people would be covered. This was thus a good, sound policy and 100% fully comprehensive.

However, Attlee's best idea and most memorable achievement was . . .

## The Welfare State

The foundations for this were laid in a very refreshing document known as the *Beverage Report*. This recommended:

(a) That coffee, tea, Bovril and other hot drinks should be available on the National Health.

(b) That everybody should wear wigs, false teeth and glasses.

(c) That every family should be allowed a maximum of 2·3 children (the Family Allowance).

(d) That everybody should have the National Health. This was so that nobody should suffer from old-fashioned ailments, e.g. scurvy, headlice, whippets, infant mortality, etc., but should have the more modern *diseases of civilisation* instead (e.g. AIDS, Herpes, Stress, etc.)

Also proposed in the Report was the Maternity Grant, or Death Grant, a very humane system whereby in cases of maternity, or death, a lump sum was paid to the victim so as to encourage him (or her) to have a baby (or bury himself). The Welfare State was thus manifestly a Good Thing, although parts of it were strongly criticised at the time, especially the provision of Sickness Benefit, which some people said was just encouraging the workers to be sick.

# *THE IRON CURTAIN*

IT was around this time that the Russians aroused considerable suspicion in the West by proceeding to put up the Iron Curtain across Europe, declaring that everything behind it was now *the East*. This was actually a Bad Thing as:

(a) It was too far West
(b) The people behind it could not see out
(c) Nobody else could see in; and
(d) It caused the Germans to be divided into two parts.

The other countries therefore immediately pronounced Russia a menace and armed themselves with the memorable *Nuclear Umbrella*. This led to the Cold War, which is still going on and is so called because anybody who starts a war with Russia is bound to catch one (c.f. Napoleon, Hitler).

# UP TO THE END OF THE FORTIES

1. If called upon to contribute to the war effort, would you have preferred to give
   (a) Blood
   (b) Sweat
   (c) Tears
   (d) Toil
   (e) Saucepans
   Tick your choice. If (a), (b) or (c), specify Blood, Sweat or Tear Group, if known. (If not known, *do not guess*.)

2. Have you ever shed Blood before? If so, give details, (e.g. Where shed, whose shed, whose Blood, if shed in service of King and Country, etc.)

3. 'Careless talk costs lives.' Discuss.

4. Using your imagination and any other means at your disposal, attempt to draw a beard on the Foe. (Compasses, pitchforks, felt tips, and garden implements may be used.)

5. Were you ever amused by Hobart's Funnies? Was anyone?

6. What makes you think that
   (a) Hitler's Diaries were written with the wrong hand?
   (b) German wartime propaganda was devised by gerbils?

7. Which of the following is more easily confused with either one of the other?
   (a) Aneurin Bevan
   (b) Ernest Bevin

   In what way did either differ from
   (a) Butskell?
   (b) Gaitler?

8. Refute the suggestion that Stafford Cripps grew watercress on his blotter.

9. 'The finest Prime Minister Britain never had.' Examine the aptness or otherwise of this remark with reference to
   (a) Baitler
   (b) Gutskell
   (c) Any other *non*-Prime Ministers you can think of.

10. Place in order of Historical Irrelevance:
   (a) King Zog of Albania
   (b) King Boris of Bulgaria
   (c) The Belisha Beacon
   (d) The Tanganyika Groundnut Scheme

*The White Man's Burden*

# Part 5

# The Fifties —
# A Drab Decade

The Fifties were a somewhat drab decade to begin with, due to Austerity. This was a policy invented by Cripps, a vegetarian, who was himself somewhat drab and austere and was once mistaken by Churchill for God, whereas in fact he was only the Chancellor of the Exchequer.

The Fifties were also memorable for:

(i) *Loss of Empire*. This was on account of the Wind of Change, which was blowing through the colonies and making life very uncomfortable for the British people there, since they had forgotten to bring any warm clothes with them. The Loss of Empire was, however, really a Good Thing, as it encouraged the natives to be more independent, and thus allowed the British to stop carrying the White Man's Burden.

(ii) *The Trial of Lady Chatterley*. This excited great public interest and was held in 1959 on the grounds that parts of her were obscene.

(iii) *Invention of teenagers*. This first occurred in America, and was the result of Rock and Roll being discovered by the memorable crooner and only American King, Elvis Presley. Shortly afterwards, teenagers were discovered in Britain too, and soon became so numerous that coffee bars had to be built to put them in.

(iv) *The Population Explosion*. Also, towards the end of the decade, the population exploded.

# CHAPTER ONE

# *BURGESSANMACLEAN: A DOUBLY BAD THING*

No sooner had the Fifties begun than there took place the shock defection to the East of the traitorous British double agent Burgessanmaclean, who, it was found, had for some years been guilty of leaking highly sensitive classified advertisements to the Russians.

Burgessanmaclean had first become treacherous at Cambridge during the Thirties, due to the Climate of Treason, which was then at its height (c.f. the emergence in that same period of the well-known fellow-traveller and double poet Audenanisherwood). This caused him to join the Apostles, some brilliant young men who were all very keen on treachery and met once a week to read each other poems and papers on it. Burgessanmaclean, however, outshone them all and was soon quite notorious all over Cambridge for his treachery, as whenever he was offered the choice of betraying his friends or his country, he would always betray his country.

Having taken a double first in espionage, he then became a top-ranking double diplomat and Russian sleeper and all through the Forties secretly slept for the Russians, until one day he overslept and was late for work, thus arousing the suspicions of his superiors (whom all this time he had been doublecrossing). To avoid capture, he then hid himself in the diplomatic bag and was accidentally posted to Moscow. Here for some years he lived the lonely life of an exile, before eventually dying of a surfeit of *dachas*, Fortnum and Mason caviare and double Vodkas. Burgessanmaclean was thus a Doubly Bad Thing, and thereafter was popularly known as the First or Second Man, or Men. (Being a Double, he counted as two.)

# *THE McCARTHY WITCHHUNTS*

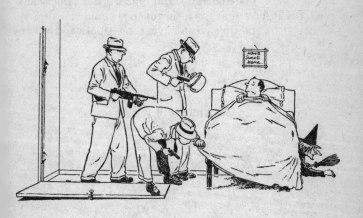

EVEN before the Burgessanmaclean Affair, there had been widespread concern about the Red Peril, and in America this had led to the memorable McCarthy Witchhunts. These were also a Bad Thing and were caused by Senator Joseph McCarthy, the infamous American McCarthyite, who around this time invented the following two important rules:

(i) That everything was either *American* (e.g. the Flag, Mom's Apple Pie, etc.) or conversely *Unamerican* (e.g. Russians, Witches, Martians, etc.); and
(ii) That everybody was either Red, or (preferably) Dead.

Having made these vital distinctions, McCarthy then issued the memorable *Apple Pie Order*, ordering that every bed in the land be inspected by Federal Agents in case there was anybody Unamerican hiding under it (such as a Red, or Witch). Each bed was then declared either (a) An Apple Pie Bed, or (b) A Hotbed of Subversion, and any Unamerican person found underneath it instantly tried, found guilty and burnt at the stake. Though this was in fact very undemocratic and unfair, the Americans tolerated it for a time, as it meant they could sleep safely in their beds and thus go on having the American Dream.

## CHAPTER THREE

## *THE NEW ELIZABETHAN AGE*

DURING the early part of the Fifties, enormous enthusiasm was shown by the British people for a Second Elizabethan Age, the First Elizabethan Age having been generally considered a success. George VI therefore died, thus making way, by overwhelming popular demand, for the glorious *Coronation of Queen Elizabeth II*.

At the time of her accession, Queen Elizabeth had been up a gum tree in Kenya. However, on hearing that she was Queen, she nimbly and graciously descended to the throne, to scenes of unprecedented popular rejoicing. Indeed, so splendid and glittering was her coronation that a Street was named after it in Granada. (The Coronation is also especially relevant and memorable as it coincided with the intrepid British ascent of Everest, by Hunt, Edmund, Hilary, the Abominable Snowman and the memorable Sherka Tenzing. *See below.*)

Although it was the world's highest mountain peak, Everest had never before been scaled, since no-one was sure if it was there. However, on discovering that it was definitely there, an intrepid British team led by Hunt immediately intrepidly scaled it, thus causing one of the highpoints of the Fifties. (The Ascent of Everest is particularly memorable and relevant as it coincided with the Descent to the Throne of Queen Elizabeth II. *See above.*)

CHAPTER FOUR

# *THE SUEZ CRISIS*

AFTER the Pharaohs, nothing of historical importance had happened in Egypt for thousands of years, other than droughts, floods, plagues of locusts, occasional Gordon Riots, etc.; and so in 1956 Colonel Nasser decided to cause the Suez Crisis. Egypt thus immediately re-entered History.

The Suez Affair began when Nasser, in flagrant breach of all agreed international procedure, placed his thumb on Eden's windpipe. This was a very Bad Thing, since the windpipe was of enormous strategic importance and was needed to convey vital supplies of oxygen to the P.M.'s brain. Nasser's action thus caused Eden to suffer an attack of post-colonial delusions of grandeur and so to accidentally order the invasion of Suez. (Historians believe that Eden at this time may have confused Nasser with Hitler, owing to the fact that both men were foreigners and wore a moustache. Alternatively, Nasser may have mistaken Eden for the well-known hat of the same name.)

The invasion of Suez has often been considered a military failure, and was quite difficult for the Army as it took place in very poor visibility, due to the Twilight of Empire; also, the British soldiers could not shoot too many Egyptians during it, in case of alienating world opinion. Fortunately, however, around this time Russia threatened to drop a bomb on London, thus causing Eden to become sane again and cancel the whole operation. The troops were thus withdrawn and the Egyptians, wrongly claiming a diplomatic victory, celebrated according to ancient Arab custom by sinking all the ships in the Suez Canal.

The importance of the Suez Affair has always been greatly exaggerated by Britain's detractors, as it was really only a minor disaster.

CHAPTER FIVE

## THE AFFLUENT SOCIETY

FOLLOWING the resignation of Eden, Harold Macmillan, although he really belonged to the Edwardian Era, was made Prime Minister of Britain, thus inaugurating the Macmillan Era. During this period great peace and prosperity descended on the land, causing Britain under Macmillan to be frequently compared with the Merrie Englande of Yore, only without the witch-burnings, Bubonic Plague, etc.

On coming to power, Macmillan immediately became memorable by inventing a number of useful household gadgets, including the vacuum cleaner, dishwasher, refrigerator and hovercraft, all of which were soon in everyday use in homes throughout the land. Also, in order to show that Austerity was over, he formed a society known as the Affluent Society. This was a Good Thing, and everybody was allowed to belong to it except the Old Age Pensioners, who did not realise that Austerity was a thing of the past and were thus still suffering from it. Such was the new national mood of well-being at this time that the people went in for a very ostentatious way of eating known as *conspicuous consumption*; as a result, many grew to be enormously fat and thus came to be known as the Gross National Product.

*The Gross National Product*

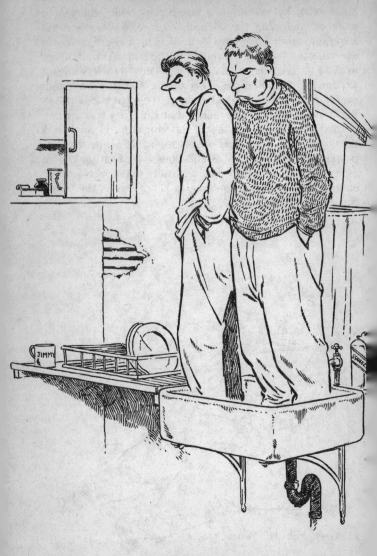

*Angry young men*

Throughout his term of office, Macmillan was extremely memorable for his memorable sayings, and on one famous occasion remarked that the people of Britain had 'never had it so good'. This phrase was considered so apt and statesmanlike that all the people immediately believed it (except the Old Age Pensioners). Macmillan was therefore gratefully and affectionately dubbed 'Supermac' (but not by the Old Age Pensioners), and everybody was contented except for . . .

## The Angry Young Men

These consisted of some revolting and irascible playwrights, who had never had proper parents, as they were the children of the Welfare State. This had made them very spoilt and bad-tempered and caused them to write Angry Young Plays, or Kitchen Sink Dramas, so called because the idea had come to them one day while they were doing the washing up. Fortunately none of these are memorable today, with the exception of *Look Back in Anger*, which enjoyed a very long run at the Royal Court as it was so popular with the Queen.

# Part 6

# *The Sixties – A Swinging Decade*

During this turbulent decade, everybody in Britain was thrown into complete convulsions, as they had lost an Empire but had not found a role (except for Rock and Roll), and also because they were having the *British Social Revolution*. This memorable upheaval was caused by a number of causes, the most notable being:

(i) *The Affluent Society*. Though originally a Good Thing, this had got quite out of control, as now even the workers were demanding the Quality of Life (e.g. holidays, dishwashers, life peerages, etc.)

(ii) *The Mass Media*. The worst of these was television, which had been invented in the Twenties by Lord Reith, the memorable educationalist and Reith-Lecturer; this was followed by advertising and colour supplements, which were exploiting the masses and causing them to suffer from Mass Hysteria.

(iii) *The Young Generation*. Due to the recent abolition of National Service, Britain's youth had nothing to do but grow its hair, wear miniskirts and advocate Love and Peace, which was plainly a Bad Thing.

(iv) *The Spirit of the Times*. This occurred throughout the decade and particularly in 1968, thus giving rise to rampant Hedonism and Permissiveness (see p. 82). These were very expensive and eventually led to the Balance of Payments Deficit, the Sick Pound, Runaway Inflation, etc.

Such was the general ferment and turmoil at this time that Britain eventually ceased to have Great Power status, and so could only lead the world in fashion, pop music and football. The Sixties were thus in the end a Bad Thing, and only made the Seventies more inevitable.

## CHAPTER ONE

## *THE GREAT WAVE OF PERMISSIVENESS*

E VER since Ancient Times, the British People had stuck to Victorian Morality, according to which nobody was allowed to get married out of wedlock, or expose their legs in public, except for artistic reasons. However, during the Sixties, as there was already a social revolution going on, it was decided in certain quarters to have the Sexual Revolution too. Consequently, a Great Wave of Permissiveness engulfed the land, eventually swamping the capital, which was duly pronounced Swinging London* (or

*Swinging London*. This was greatly exaggerated by the media and probably did not exist at all except in Carnaby Street, which was fortunate, as if it had, it would almost certainly have been a Bad Thing. Since it did not exist, it was a Good Thing and prompted many foreign tourists to flock to Britain to see if it existed or not, thus causing *Invisible Exports*. Though invisible, these definitely did exist and were extremely popular with the top men at the Treasury.

*Invisible Exports*

Sodom and Gomorrah), and anybody who did not join in it was termed a *square*. (It is not known exactly where Permissiveness originated; however, probably it was in Sweden or Denmark, since everything was very open there, e.g. the Open Prison, Open Sandwich, etc.)

Fortunately, the Wave of Permissiveness was bound to be defeated in the end since:

(a) London was full of squares;
(b) It scandalised all Right-Thinking People, thus caus-ing them to revive a cruel seventeenth-century punish-ment known as the Puritan Backlash.

### The Property Boom

At the same time there was a Property Boom in Britain, which was caused by the discovery that many of Britain's slums were in quite bad condition, having been reduced to rubble by the Luftwaffe during the war. The planners therefore decided to pull the old slums down and build new, taller ones known as *Tower Blocks* in their place, e.g. Tower Hamlets, Ronan Point, etc. These were much tidier-looking, and did not need to have bombs dropped on them since they were designed to collapse or blow up of their own accord.

# CHAPTER TWO

## *THE BAY OF PIGS*

IN 1960, much excitement had been caused in America by the rise to power of John F. Kennedy, who, being young, good-looking, romantic and full of vigour, had won the hearts of the people and easily become President of the United States.

In 1962, however, hearing that the Cuban Leader Fidel Castro was also young, good-looking and in addition, *bearded* (and thus a dangerous revolutionary), Kennedy immediately took steps to destabilise him, e.g. by sending him a box of exploding cigars and (when this failed) ordering Cuba to be invaded by an army of Cubans at the memorable *Bay of Pigs*. This, however, also failed, since the pigs quickly raised the alarm, thus causing the invading Cubans to defeat themselves.

The Bay of Pigs was thus a Bad Thing and was rapidly succeeded by . . .

### The Cuban Missiles Crisis

A major figure on the world stage at this time was the memorable Russian leader Nikita Kruschev. As well as being renowned for his heavy drinking and coarse peasant wit, Kruschev was also addicted to gambling, and one of his favourite games was *Call My Bluff*, which he played with Kennedy for several weeks in 1962. This consisted of the Russian leader threatening to send some missiles to Cuba as a present for Castro; Kennedy then had to guess whether he would or not.

Having played this game and lost, Kennedy decided to invent a game of his own called *Whose Finger On The Button*

In this, he and Kruschev both sat at their desks with their hands poised above a little red button, and the winner was whoever pressed it first. Fearing that he might lose, however, Kruschev refused to play and was disqualified, thus showing himself to be a Weak Man and a Bad Sport. N.B. This game was also known as the *Balance of Terror* and although considered dangerous at the time, was quite safe really, owing to the existence of the *Hot Line*. This was a direct telephone link between Washington and the Kremlin, and meant that if either leader felt he might be about to drop a bomb or start a nuclear war, he could ring the other one up and let him know first. The Hot Line was thus a Good Thing, as it helped to preserve world peace (and saved having to go through the operator).

# CHAPTER THREE

# *THE PROFUMO AFFAIR*

IN the early Sixties, finding that there had not been a major political scandal for some years, the British Public suddenly conceived an inordinate craving for sensational disclosures, and revelations of corruption in High Places. In order to satisfy this, a Succession of Scandals therefore took place in Britain, consisting of the Vaseline Case, the George Blake Case, the Duchess of Argyll Divorce Case, and culminating in 1963 in the utterly memorable *Profumo Affair* (or Russian Naval Attaché Case).

This occurred at *Cliveden*, a suburb of Swinging London which was very famous at the time for the famous romps, fancy dress parties and Roman orgies which went on there, many of them attended by top Cabinet Ministers, Russian diplomats and other assorted low-lifes of the day, e.g. Captain Ivanov, Douglas Fairbanks Jr., the Man in the Iron Mask, etc. (otherwise known collectively as the *Neasden Set.*) To one such party, the Secretary of State for War, John Profumo, had been invited, and was just relaxing beside the swimming pool when he unexpectedly fell in with Christine Keeler.

This incident so embarrassed the government that (a) A Denning Report was written about it (by Lord Denning); (b) Macmillan turned grey overnight, immediately becoming sixty-nine years old and thus an Elder Statesman.

The Profumo Affair thus caused the downfall of the Macmillan Ministry. (Macmillan however always denied this, privately maintaining that he had been brought down by *Two Tarts*.)

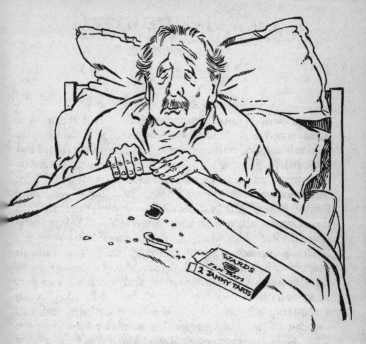

*brought down by two tarts*

# CHAPTER FOUR

## *CHINA IN THE SIXTIES*

IN Ancient Times, Imperial China had been very advanced and civilised and was the first nation ever to invent fireworks, bureaucracy and Woks; afterwards, however, it had become more and more irrelevant, gradually ceasing to have any memorable history at all apart from interminable opium wars, Boxer Rebellions, etc., until finally the peasants became so disgusted that they decided to abolish it altogether and have the *People's Republic of China* instead. This was a Good Thing as it led to the Sino-Soviet Split, and was the cause of the first memorable modern Chinaman, viz. Chairman Mao Tse-Tung.

Mao was a very strong leader and was always in very good health, which he proved by performing many astounding gymnastic feats, e.g. his great leaps and long marches. The most memorable of these, however, was when he swam the Yangtse River, which was very dangerous owing to its powerful revolutionary currents. This astonished the world and so inspired the Chinese people that it immediately caused the Chinese Cultural Revolution (which thenceforward progressed by leaps and bounds).

### The Cultural Revolution

Besides being inscrutable, the Chinese have always been a very cheerful industrious people, and during the Cultural Revolution they became more cheerful and smiling than ever, on account of Mao's great wisdom and benevolence. However, a few landowners and intellectuals did not seem

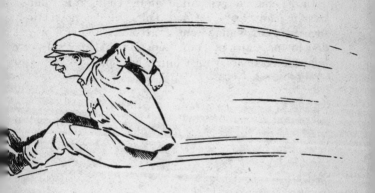

to be smiling very much, so to encourage them to smile more, Mao very wisely and benevolently set them to work on the land for twenty-four hours a day. This helped them to rethink their position and so become cheerful and industrious like everyone else, and was thus a very successful policy except when the landowners, intellectuals, etc., died of it.

In the end, however, although the Cultural Revolution was in many ways a Good Thing, it did not entirely succeed in eliminating want, greed or corruption. This was due to the Gang of Four, and also to Human Nature (which unfortunately the Chinese have too).

# CHAPTER FIVE

# *BRITAIN IN THE DOLDRUMS*

DURING the Macmillan era, Britain had sunk deeper and deeper into Economic Difficulties, due to:

(a) *The Economic Miracle*. (There had not been an economic miracle.)

(b) *The Thirteen Years of Tory Misrule*. These were caused by too much Grouse Moor Leadership, e.g. Sir Alec Douglas Home, who wore tweeds and spoke without moving his lips; this was Irrelevant and thus a Bad Thing.

(c) *Failure to enter Europe*. For some years, Britain had been attempting to join the Common Market, but each time had been prevented by General de Gaulle's nose.

(d) *The Stop-Go Spiral* (or *Cycle*). Very few people knew what this was; but whatever it was, it was bad for the country, and so Top Economists insisted it should Go (or alternatively, Stop).

A general election was therefore held, and universal public rejoicing broke out when *Harold Wilson* was voted Prime Minister, by a slender majority.

## *The Wilson Years*

One of the reasons for Wilson's popularity was undoubtedly his pipe and his raincoat, and also his policies. He was, however, quite a confusing Prime Minister, and very crafty and pragmatic, so that it was hard to tell if he was Right or Left or not. One example of this was his Incomes Policy, which he disagreed with at first and did not have; later, he changed his mind and declared that he had secretly had one all the time really, thus showing his skilled statecraft. He was also popular for his informal style, which he showed by holding Cabinet meetings in a cabinet in his kitchen (the Kitchen Cabinet) and ordering all his ministers to wear shirt sleeves and smoke pipes like him (thus causing the memorable Smoke-Filled Rooms.)

During the Wilson Years, Wilson made many innovations, including his very generous policy of giving a Wilson Honour to his friends or anybody else who needed one. Many top entertainers benefited from this, such as Lords Kagan, Gannex, Yarwood, the Baron Knights. (Wilson was quite a good entertainer himself and was sometimes known as the Houdini of Huyton, on account of his many tricks and contortions.) The most memorable of his innovations, however, was the White Heat of Technology,

*The Molten Bicycle*

which was done by men in white coats, or *Boffins*, and rapidly transformed everything, including Society. The White Heat of Technology was thus a Good Thing, and led to the invention of the Molten Bicycle.

### Wilson devalues the Pound

Wilson was very eager to solve Britain's economic problems, and one of the first things he did was to hold the Hundred Days of Action, when all the ministers thought up interesting new policies and the civil servants thought up very detailed reasons why none of them would work. But this did not halt Britain's economic decline, and so in 1967 he decided to devalue the Pound, as it had become far too valuable.*

Many ordinary people were very confused by this, until Wilson made a memorable speech on television pointing out that everybody would still have a Pound In Their Pocket, after which they were very relieved and could see that it was all right and they would not be international paupers after all. (There was never any danger of this really, because of the International Monetary Fund, a very wealthy charitable foundation run by the Club of Ten, a firm of ten very rich gnomes in Zurich.)

### Two Memorable Diarists

A great deal of light was shed on the inner workings of government at this time by two diarists: Mr Wilson's poetic wife Mary (Gladys), and the memorable Cabinet Minister Richard Crossman. The Crossman Diaries, however, contained so many embarrassing revelations that they had to be written posthumously after Crossman's death due to the Thirty Year Rule, or doctrine of Collective Cabinet Responsibility. (This rule states that (i) Every Cabinet Minister must always behave responsibly; and (ii) That if a Cabinet Minister does anything irresponsible, no other Cabinet Minister must say so until thirty years later.)

*A Strong Pound is usually a Bad Thing as it makes British Goods very expensive for foreigners, and forces Britain to become a Net Importer (of foreign nets).

*Whitehall Mandarin*

The Crossman Diaries are particularly relevant as they show that the Wilson Government could never have done anything very Left-Wing in Britain anyway, owing to the *Whitehall Mandarins*.

# Chapter Six

## *THE SIX-DAY WAR*

WHILE the Wilson Years were going on in Britain, various wars were being conducted abroad, the most notable being the Vietnam War (caused by the Domino Theory, and eventually lost by the Americans due to the media, drugs, Flower Power, Campus Riots, etc.), and (shorter, and thus more easily memorable) the *Six-Day War*. This occurred in the Middle East and was exceptionally inevitable on account of the Egyptians (Arabs) led by Nasser, and the Israelis (Israelis), led by God. The events of the Six-Day War are quite straightforward, as can be seen by the following somewhat *rationalised* table:

---

DAY 1 Egypt *declares all-out war on* Israel; Saudi *troops sent to* Jordan.

DAY 2 Israel *declares all-out war on* Egypt; *destroys Egyptian Airforce in* Egypt; *bombs Iraqi planes in* Jordan; *bombs Syrian planes (in* Syria*)*.

DAY 3 Jordan *invades* Israel.

DAY 4 Israel *invades* Israel, *thus defeating* Jordan.

DAY 5 Israel *invades* Syria, *thus defeating everybody*.

DAY 6 *All Arab forces annihilated. Peace with Arabs.*

---

The Six-Day War was thus a heroic and decisive victory for Israel, and was one of the chief causes of the memorable Israeli war-hero, Moshe Dayan.

# CHAPTER SEVEN

# *THE SPACE RACE*

THROUGHOUT the Sixties America and Russia were both very busy trying to conquer Space, since it was the Final Frontier (the Americans having by now crossed all the other ones). This led to the Space Race, which the Americans easily won in 1969, when the U.S. astronaut Neil Armstrong successfully landed on the Moon and did a Giant Leap for Mankind there. (The success of the American Space effort was very largely due to the superiority of their crews, who all wore crewcuts and had the *Right Stuff*; whereas the Russian spaceships were mostly manned by dogs, mice or hamsters.)

The Space Race had a number of good results, not least for the astronauts themselves, many of whom became quite otherworldly and had nervous breakdowns, or became Born Again Christians and were thus able to run for the Presidency.

Another good result was Satellite Communications; these were very useful as they could bring the people all the latest news of any wars, earthquakes, famines or other natural disasters that might be happening around the world. The growth of satellite technology also led to the invention of the *global village* by the memorable U.S. Sheriff and guru Marshal McCluhan; (this, however, was later found to be impractical, as the cottages on the bottom half of the globe kept dropping off).

The conquest of Space was thus on the whole a Good Thing and not a waste of money at all, and may one day result in a cure for the Common Cold (although this has not happened yet).

*The Global Village*

# CHAPTER EIGHT

## END OF THE SIXTIES

### Collapse of the Wilson Government

ALTHOUGH he was very good at Party Unity, Wilson was a bungler in foreign affairs and consequently could never solve the Rhodesian Crisis. (This was caused in 1965 by Ian Smith declaring he was independent and Britain declaring he was not.) Also, people kept asking him the Irish Question, which he could not answer properly. In the meantime at home there had been harsh budgets, Stirling Crises, strikes, etc., and many rich people had been made to tighten their belts and were now complaining of *squeaking pips*. (Wilson also lost further popularity at this time by threatening to reform the Lords, which he tried to do by creating a wave of Labour Peers and then ordering them to abolish themselves.)

All of which gave rise to such discontent among the people that at the memorable June election of 1970, Wilson was utterly defeated and Edward Heath became Prime Minister of Britain instead, thus finally putting an end to Swinging London, the Permissive Society, the Sixties and All That, and forcing Wilson to flee to the Scilly Isles (a remote branch of the political wilderness not far from Cornwall).

# TEST PAPER IV

## *UP TO THE END OF THE SIXTIES*

1. In what sense can Macmillan be said to have stolen Gaitskell's clothes?
   What was Gaitskell doing at the time?

2. Investigate Macmillan's claim to have 'juggled with five balls in the air', outlining any anatomical reason why this might be impossible.

3. With the help of tracing paper, draw a polite veil over
   (a) The Duchess of Argyll
   (b) Lady Chatterley
   (c) The G.P.O. Tower

4. By means of grappling irons, ropes and tackle, etc., attempt to bridge
   (a) The Generation Gap
   (b) The Trade Gap
   (c) The Watford Gap

5. Using your calculator, estimate
   (a) The height of the Cold War
   (b) The Age of Aquarius
   (c) The chest and waist measurements of the Gross National Product

6. What caused the Property Boom? Speculate wildly.

7. Compare and contrast
   (a) The Giant Hogweed
   (b) Tiny Tim
   (c) Little Richard

8. Consider the influence of the Rhythm Method on the Beat Generation.

9. How might Labour's political fortunes have been affected if
   (a) Lord Kagan had invented the mini-skirt?
   (b) Harold Wilson had been declared a smokeless zone?

10. Calculate the number of Small Steps in a Giant Leap, allowing for the effects of Zero Gravity.

# Part 7

## *The Seventies – A Bleak Decade*

With the death of the Sixties, we come at last to the Seventies and thus to the beginning of *recent* (Relevant) Twentieth-Century History. This period is nothing but a great number of hijackings, hostage-takings, industrial disputes, go-slows and droughts, most of which, though best forgotten, are (unfortunately) too recent not to be Memorable.

One of the only Good Things to come out of the Seventies was North Sea Oil (many people, however, dispute this and claim that North Sea Oil was first discovered in the *Forties*). Another quite Good Thing was that many of the Hippies and drop-outs who had grown their hair long in the Sixties now decided to cut it, thus causing the memorable *Barber Boom*.

# CHAPTER ONE

## *HEATH AND THE HEATHMEN*

ALTHOUGH he was quite able and statesmanlike and came from Broadstairs, Edward Heath never became popular as Prime Minister of Britain, as instead of being married, he devoted his spare time to sailing and playing the organ. His teeth also counted against him, since whenever he smiled, he showed the *Unacceptable Face of Capitalism*.

During his term of office Heath also achieved wide popular unpopularity by means of his unpopular policies. These consisted of:

(i) *Redrawing the County Boundaries*, thus covering the country with imaginary lines and artificial administrative entities, e.g. Humberside, Avon, Gwent, etc. This confused the rate-payers and increased the size of local government bureaucrats.

(ii) *Legalising industrial relations between consenting adults.* This was to curb the power of the Unions, and was accordingly unpopular with them.

(iii) *Decimating the coinage.* This was done on D-Day 1971, and was not fair on the Old Folk. (They could not handle the Change.)

In spite of not being popular, Heath was a forceful character and very ambitious, and one of his lifelong ambitions was to conduct the London Symphony Orchestra. In the end, he achieved this, since he was Prime Minister now and nobody could really stop him.

### Britain enters Europe

Heath spoke very bad French; he was, however, very European-minded, and always believed the nation's future lay in Europe, as it would be so much handier for buying Britain's groceries. He therefore immediately asked if Britain could join the *Common Market*. This consisted of the memorable *Six*, each of whom sat around a table in Brussels, where they traded beef, dairy produce, Brussels Sprouts and Rabies, and took it in turns to be the Sick Man of Europe. (Even before this, Britain had been steadily moving closer to Europe, in order to make up for the Loss of Empire, and also so as to avoid having to build the Channel Tunnel, or so-called French Connection.)

One reason for Britain's successful entry into Europe at this time was the collapse of the French Resistance; this had been chiefly caused by General de Gaulle (see p. 91), who was renowned for always resisting everything and who had recently died of natural causes (having obstinately resisted all attempts to assassinate him).

Following British membership of the Common Market, many changes took place in Britain. Over a long period, the day was gradually lengthened to include twenty-four

*The Sick Man of Europe*

hours, thus bringing Britain into line with continental practice; also, British Summertime was introduced; this was in order to render the summer months more easily distinguishable from the rest of the year, and also to encourage managers to get out of bed earlier and thus be in a position to compete with the Germans.

Many people feared that membership of Europe would mean the end of the British Way of Life; this, however, never happened, since in spite of the Common Market, the British still drive on the Left, as distinct from the French, who drive on the Right, and the Italians, who drive on both.

## The Cod War

This war was fought between Britain on the one hand, and Iceland on the other, *wrong*, hand, and was not really relevant or memorable at all and is therefore only included here for reasons of space. The Cod War was over some disputed fishing grounds, which Iceland claimed belonged to her, but which really belonged to Britain, under the Rule Britannia, or Freedom of the Seas.* The British, however, eventually defeated the Icelanders without any difficulty, when a Royal Navy Frigate took careful aim and fired *a shot across their brows*. Thus the war was brought to a satisfactory end, leading to the utterly unmemorable and irrelevant Peace of Cod (or Codpeace).

*See 1066 AND ALL THAT.

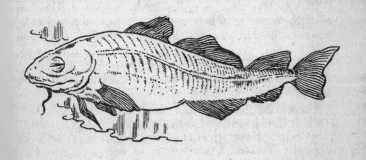

*The Peace of Cod*

CHAPTER TWO

# *THE OIL CRISIS*

THE Western World has always been very dependent on oil from the Middle East, since without it all the Western economies would gradually grind to a halt all of a sudden. This nearly occurred during the Oil Crisis of 1973, when some Arab Sheikhs, or *Opecs*, very unexpectedly raised the price of crude, in order to punish the Western leaders for not supporting them in the *Yom Kippur War* (a recent inevitable periodic Middle East flare-up). In the end the crisis was quite amicably resolved, since the Arabs agreed to moderate their demands, while in return the British Government agreed to let them shop at Harrods and buy mansions in Belgravia. For some time afterwards, however, Britain was very careful not to offend any Arab leaders, and even today, though many British people disapprove of certain Arab customs (e.g. polygamy, beheading adulterers in car-parks, etc.), they must never say so.

Some claim that the Oil Crisis was in fact a Good Thing while it lasted, since it led the introduction of the 50mph limit and was thus (temporarily) a major cause of Road Safety.

### The Winter of Discontent

Almost before the Oil Crisis was finished properly, the Black Winter or *Winter of Discontent* happened in Britain. This plunged the entire country into chaos and pitch darkness (thus causing the Black Economy), and was entirely the fault of the Unions, especially the miners, who as usual were demanding too big a slice of the National Cake (*see opposite*).

*The National Cake*

For some time before this, the Unions had been making a great nuisance of themselves by quarrelling with the Government over cooling-off periods, strike ballots, etc., and especially over the *Closed Shop*. This was a shop run by the Unions which was kept permanently closed, so nobody could enter it unless they held a Union Card, which they could only buy at the Shop (which was always Closed). The Heath Government disagreed with this and declared that the Closed Shop was illegal unless it was opened, thus allowing the workers to enter it, after which it could quite legally be Closed again (the so-called post-entry Closed Shop). This, however, so incensed the Unions that they immediately unleashed a series of strikes, shutdowns, snowstorms, blackouts and exorbitant wage demands, until eventually Britain became so ungovernable that Heath was forced to go to the country in order to find out who was running it, whereupon, finding it was not him, he resigned in a huff.

# CHAPTER THREE

# *AMERICA IN THE DOGHOUSE: THE WATERGATE SCANDAL*

R ICHARD NIXON was a Bad President. Indeed, he was so bad that throughout his Presidency nobody would buy a used car from him, on account of his untrustworthy appearance and five o'clock shadow. Nixon's aides were also very bad and were notorious around Washington for the Dirty Tricks they played on people, e.g. burglarising their apartments, steaming open the Washington Post, and paying bribes with laundered money from a laundry in Mexico.

Nixon was obsessed with secrecy and always liked to know of any secret plots that might be hatching. He therefore arranged for a group of his henchmen to dress up as plumbers and eavesdrop on his rivals, while all the time pretending to check for leaks. This led to the memorable Watergate Break-In, which Nixon ordered in such a secret way that later he claimed even he did not know about it. (There were in fact many things he did not know about, due to the *Wall Around the President*; this had been very cunningly built by his aides so as to prevent anyone telling him anything he might not want to hear, e.g. that there was a Wall Around the President [which he did not know about either].)

In the end, however, Nixon's paranoia was his own undoing, since while secretly bugging all his political enemies, he also secretly bugged himself by mistake, thus causing the Watergate Tapes. These consisted entirely of deleted expletives and were so incriminating that Nixon was put on trial and finally publicly impaled in full view of the nation.


### The Salt Talks

During the Nixon Era there also occurred the policy of Detente, which consisted of Nixon's memorable Foreign Policy adviser Henry Kissinger flying all over the world making overtures to the Russians. This encouraged the Russians to make overtures to the West (the first time this had happened since Tchaikovsky's well-known overture of 1812), and so led to the *Salt Talks*.

The Salt Talks took place in Geneva or Helsinki, and many important issues were discussed there, especially arms control. This was very necessary at this time, since America and Russia together had enough nuclear weapons to destroy the world several times over, when most people felt that once would be ample. Also, both sides were very concerned about Mutual Assured Destruction. According to this theory, if either Superpower unleashed a First Strike, the other would immediately unleash a First Strike too, and so all the weapons would be wasted. This was considered to be such a Bad Thing that both sides promised never to let it happen except by accident, or if they went Mad.

Since the Salt Talks, the Western leaders have alway

tried to continue the dialogue with the Soviet Union. This, however, is often very difficult, owing to the Soviet Premiers, who are mostly very old and tired and hard of hearing, and insist on remaining in office long after they are dead. Thus even today the two sides are still separated by a *Yawning Gap*. (This can be defined as the distance between two politicians.)

*The Yawning Gap*

# CHAPTER FOUR

# *THE WILSON YEARS AGAIN*

FOLLOWING the defeat of the Heath Government at the miners' election, Harold Wilson had taken office again and there had thus been a brief recurrence of the *Wilson Years* in Britain. These, however, were only notable for the Social Contract (designed by the memorable architect Jack Jones) and Runaway or Galloping Inflation, and were soon brought to an end when Wilson unexpectedly resigned, due to mysterious circumstances.

In spite of his sunny disposition, Wilson's successor Callaghan did not succeed in becoming memorable at all, as at this time the people were far more interested in the Thorpe Affair. This occurred when the former Liberal leader was put on trial at the Old Bailey, after admitting a past affair with a dog.

# CHAPTER FIVE

# *TWO WEAK PRESIDENTS*

MEANWHILE, since Richard Nixon had been a Bad President, the American people had very carefully chosen two Good Men to succeed him. This was unwise as it turned out, since both men, though Good, proved to be Weak Presidents and thus Bad as well, in a way.

The first of these was Gerald Ford. Ford, however, could not walk and chew gum at the same time and as soon as he was sworn in, immediately (a) Pardoned Nixon, and (b) Fell over, and was therefore quickly replaced by Jimmy Carter, who, it was hoped, would not fall over so much.

### The Carter Administration

Jimmy Carter came from the Deep South and is chiefly memorable for his Southern drawl and his peanut farm. Carter began by being a Good President, and was always very good to his mother, whom he placed on a pedestal in the Oval Office. He also invented jogging and Human Rights, and ordered all the White House Staff to say prayers before work each morning. Later, however, he failed to resolve the Iranian Hostage Crisis and thus became Weak instead.

# Part 8

# *The Eighties And All That*

At the start of the Eighties, a severe Recession struck Britain, causing such gloom and despondency among the people that a colourful state occasion of some kind became urgently necessary; and so the memorable Royal Wedding of Prince Charles and Lady Diana Spenser took place at St Paul's Cathedral.

This captured the imagination of the world with its pageantry, pompous circumstances and fairy-tale quality, and caused Britain to become a world leader in the manufacture of commemorative mugs, tea-towels and coffee-table books. The Royal Wedding was also particularly romantic and uplifting as it proved that true love is quite possible between persons of different age and height.

A number of other interesting events occurred during the first four years of the Eighties, including the invention of the F-Plan Diet, the Mini Metro, and the Parkinson Affair; it is, however, too early to judge if any of these will ever become memorable, and in any case, all were eclipsed by the most significant invention of the decade, namely . . .

### The Silicon Chip

This was first discovered in a Valley in California, and although of very little nutritional value, was found to be very useful technologically on account of its size (which was small). The Silicon Chip thus gave rise to the New Technology, i.e. microscopically small computers, digital alarm clocks, etc., all of which are very cheap and made in Japan and a Good Thing, except when they go wrong.

The Chip has already transformed every aspect of modern life, and nowadays no politician or planner can afford to ignore it, in case he is replaced by one.

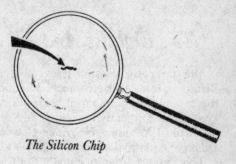

*The Silicon Chip*

# CHAPTER ONE

## *THE IRON LADY*

Shortly before the Eighties, Margaret Thatcher had confounded all her political rivals by declaring that she would never be a woman Prime Minister in her lifetime, and then, in 1979, becoming one. Thus the opposition had been thrown into complete disarray and Britain had come under the rule of the *Iron Lady*.

Thatcher was renowned for her iron will and hairstyle, and also for having very strong policies on everything. One of the strongest of these was Freedom, which she was strongly in favour of, and which she said should be freely available to anyone who could afford it (except in Iron Curtain countries such as Poland, where she thought it should be freely available to everybody). She also caused consternation:

(a) *At Brussels*, by banging the table with her fist or shopping basket, and

(b) *At home*, by her policies of Monetarism, Return to Victorian Values, No U-Turns, etc.,

thus becoming an object of terror and admiration to foreign governments, Russians, Cabinet wets and the world at large.

### The Falklands Crisis

It was not, however, until the Falklands Crisis erupted that Margaret Thatcher became most memorable. This was caused by the treacherous action of Argentina, under its tinpot dictator General Galtieri, who around this time ordered an army of scrap-metal merchants to invade the Falkland Islands, thinking Britain would not mind, since:

(a) The islands were very small and far away and populated mostly by sheep;

(b) They really belonged to Spain anyway.

The crisis was boldly faced in Britain, particularly by Thatcher herself, who instantly became very Queenly and ordered a Task Force to set sail and claim the islands back, as they were a very useful source of kelp and Britain had never seriously intended to give them up at all, but had just been pretending.

### The War

One of the most dramatic events during the Falklands War was the sinking of the Bel Grano, which was quite justifiable, since it was sailing away from the Total Exclusion Zone and thus represented a threat to the Task Force. After this, British Forces soon landed on the islands, advancing by great leaps or *yomps* to within a few miles of Port Stanley, which they later took without any difficulty, owing to the poor morale of the Argentine soldiers, who were all under-age and under-trained and suffering from *machismo*.

Although the Falklands War was a very convincing victory for the British, it was a Bad Thing in some ways as it led to Fortress Falklands, a very expensive fortress which Britain must always maintain there in case of another invasion. Also, Britain can never give up the islands now, as it would mean all the fighting had been a waste of time.

## CHAPTER TWO

## *THE GANG OF FOUR*

FOLLOWING the Labour defeat in the 1979 election, there had been a re-alignment of the Left, and a *Gang of Four* had set up a new party in the Marshy Middle Ground of Politics, a swamp on the outskirts of Westminster. They did this with the object of:

(a) Breaking the mould of British Politics
(b) Keeping Britain in Europe, retaining the Nuclear Umbrella, Volvos, Claret, etc.
(c) Introducing *Proportional Representation*. This, they claimed, would be a Good Thing as it would help them win more seats, and they could then reform the electoral system, e.g. by introducing Proportional Representation (without which they could never win any seats in the first place).

Being a new Party, the Gang of Four could not afford to have proper conferences at Brighton or Blackpool, and so had *Rolling Conferences* instead; these consisted of the members of the Gang catching trains to all parts of the country, and rather confused the electorate, who could never be sure which platform the Party was standing on.

The Gang of Four were therefore defeated at the memorable June election of 1983, and so too was the Labour Party, whose leader, Michael Foot, was especially defeated for having worn a donkey jacket at the Cenotaph. Thus Margaret Thatcher celebrated a second victory and thenceforward became more queenly than ever. (This, of course, was due to her having the Falklands Factor.)

*Marshy Middle Ground of Politics*

# Chapter Three

## *NINETEEN EIGHTY-FOUR*

With the dawn of Nineteen Eighty-Four, we arrive at the present day, and also at one of the only truly memorable Twentieth-Century *dates*.

All History becomes inconceivable beyond this point and has therefore been temporarily suspended until further notice.

# TEST PAPER V

# *UP TO THE END OF HISTORY*

1. Examine the contribution of the cheeseburger to the simultaneous deaths of one of the following:
   - (a) Groucho Marx
   - (b) Elvis Presley
   - (c) Victor the Giraffe

2. Account for the failure of Senator Edward Kennedy's 1979 presidential compaign, *but on no account mention Chappaquiddick.*

3. Would you say Margaret Thatcher was
   - (a) A strong man?
   - (b) A good Queen?
   - (c) A Bad Thing?

4. Demonstrate the horticultural futility of a Hedge against Inflation.

5. Reconstruct the capture of Port Stanley, giving due prominence to the role of the Gherkins.

6. Rearrange the letters ZBIGNIEW BWRESZINSKI to form the name of a prominent American statesman.

7. Which would you rather be savaged by:
   - (a) A Quango?
   - (b) A Womble?
   - (c) Sir Geoffrey Howe?
   - (d) A dead sheep?

8. Consider the effect of Acid Rain on:
   (a) The tree forests of Scandinavia
   (b) Denis Healey's eyebrows

9. What measure was proposed by Norman Tebbit in order to combat unemployment?
   What measure would you propose in order to combat Norman Tebbit?

10. Give the date of one or both of the following:
    (a) George Orwell
    (b) Nineteen Eighty-Four

All Futura Books are available at your bookshop or
newsagent, or can be ordered from the following
address:
Futura Books, Cash Sales Department,
P.O. Box 11, Falmouth, Cornwall.

Please send cheque or postal order (no currency), and
allow 45p for postage and packing for the first book
plus 20p for the second book and 14p for each additiona
book ordered up to a maximum charge of £1.63 in U.

Customers in Eire and B.F.P.O. please allow 45p for
the first book, 20p for the second book plus 14p per
copy for the next 7 books, thereafter 8p per book.

Overseas customers please allow 75p for postage an
packing for the first book and 21p per copy for each
additional book.